OM Poems

Self-Meditation

and

Science and Spirituality in Balance

by
Dr. Tushar K. Ray

PublishAmerica
Baltimore

First printing

ISBN: 1-4137-2871-5
PUBLISHED BY PUBLISHAMERICA, LLLP
www.publishamerica.com
Baltimore

Printed in the United States of America

OM Poems is dedicated to my beloved wife Mukta Mala Ray, who has been a source of inspiration for me all our married life. Her persistent selfless service for the health and well being of the members of our family offered me the solace and confidence that I needed for this exclusive time-consuming work. But for her love, encouragement, and understanding it would not have been possible for me to take this spiritual journey. Forever I remain grateful to her for her relentless love and care for all concerned.

OM Poems is also dedicated to our first grandchild, Lucy Mala Ray, born to Amit and Jessica. May Lucy's life be harmonious with the spirit of *OM Poems* and resonate with the newly emerging world of holistic consciousness lurking just ahead of us.

I gratefully acknowledge the all-out help of my dear friend, Alan Schneider. Himself being a writer, Alan has been whole heartedly supportive of my creative activities ever since we met. We have had many enjoyable discussions together on various poems of mine relative to some of his similar experiences. He helped me in editing some of my recent poems with his spiritual insight and proficiency in English language. In addition, Alan helps me out quite frequently with his knowledge and expertise in computer usage.

I am also thankful to my son Ashim for being a thoughtful and enthusiastic reader of my poems over the years. I am aware that some of my poems motivated him to make a serious spiritual journey on his own. It is indeed a great joy to see him growing in this holistic maturity!

OM Poems I:

On Science and Spirituality

Dynamic Duo

Healthy foods coupled with healthy thoughts
Make the best soups for our Soul:
The former for the body
And the latter for the mind
And together they lift us to our cherished goals

Thoughts materialized make the body
And remain hidden in the subconscious
But surface again as thoughts in time
Influencing decisions by our conscious

Thus the conscious and the subconscious
Is our dynamic duo
And eternal companion of the Soul
That engages in action for our soul to experience
Leading to the freedom in action as the goal

-- 5/14/2002; Phoenix, AZ 85008

9

Endless Dream

The other day the joy I felt in my pleasant dream
Was an episode I couldn't discount
Since, so vivid was my feeling as if I was awaken
Which made me arrive at this firm conclusion, that
All feelings must stem from the subconscious plane
Where all our desires display their eternal games
That mirrors upon the body in waking and dreaming
Creating an identical bodily feeling
Independent of the state of our enacting consciousness

So, human life is more like an endless dream
And is essentially an endless game of the mind
Where we experience good or bad at random in a chain
When, good things bring joy, so we relish them
Gross things bring grief, so we do bury them
While scary ones make us helpless giving real pains
So, our rapport with different things of life in dreams
Are as real as those in our waking schemes

Hence I salute you affectionately, oh my mind
As you made me realize a great lesson in life
That our mind is in the middle of a constant game
And, controlling our own mind can we control the same
By way of removing the negativities of mind
Following the time-tested practice of Yoga and Meditation
So, the name of the game today is 'Tame Your own Mind'
In order to achieve a life of relentless bliss
And look for the good days on earth looming ahead,
Not far away from where we are at present, indeed!

--Phoenix, AZ; 1/17/2002

Spirituality

In reality we are the invincible Spirit
Shining through our amazing intellect
And as evidenced from our deep inner feelings
In our thoughts, actions and dealings
The power of mighty Spirit is only reflected

The Spirit reigns in the throne of our heart
Feeling all acts as the feedback witness, while
The intellect dwells in the crown of our head
Serving as the guide of our true providence.
Intellect shines in the light of our knowledge
This reflects often in our emotional colors
And shining assorted rays of typical nature
Makes people discernible one from the other

The problems in life that we all encounter
Occur due to neglect of our spiritual nature
And too much attention to the lust and greed
Makes us forget our truest feature

Hence happiest way to live in this world
As has been noted by all Yogi Masters
Is to get our senses first melted into intellect, and
Melt the intellect in turn in our "I-consciousness"
That naturally culminates into vast "God-consciousness"
Thus feeling God's power in His Nature everywhere
We could live happily in His enchanting universe

-- Phoenix, AZ; 4/4/2002

11

Holistic Yogic Awareness
(Science Concurs With Spirituality)

The single primal power of this universe is flowing all around us
And manifested as multiple objects in numerous names and forms
Making them look and feel so different on the surface
Yet deep down inside, truly, they are one and the same

The ignorance as a dark drape has blocked our vision
Averting the rays of intellect from razing the layers of MAYA
And most of us are so trapped in this mode all life long
That regardless of sufferings we stay put in this mortal domain

Moreover, the area past this common path is so radically rare
That most people feel insecure to step into that sphere, but
Ignoring that daring option as unreal figment of the mind
Is a lack of novelty and empathy on the part of any mankind

It's this unseen domain that holds the key to the unity of things
Being a field of pure energy as the source of colors and forms
And a realm of pure love where our firm intellect stays as a bystander
When holistic aspect of the object of study comes to view utterly clear

Then, we do see the basic unity in spite of all the duality around
As we get the nondual view of things from without and within
When the intellect and feeling stay busy holding a balanced position
While helping us to see the reality by offering full cooperation

The mind becomes free at last after direct experience of this truth
That there is only one Great intellect pervading our Universe
And all living things are the diverse lexis of this only Great One
In who melts our own intellect being one with this grand Universe

Like a drop of rain happily melts in the realm of a boundless ocean
So does an observer drop her identity becoming this Universe again!
Only then do we finally realize this holisticity of holistic things
When a part becomes the whole again being one with its own essence

--Tempe, AZ 85281, June 2, 2003

OM Universal Mother OM
(Science concurs with spirituality)

This Primordial Energy—this vast mystical power!
Is indeed an endless ocean of creative order
And the only building material of this incredible universe
Including this changing body that we inhabit

This body of ours we owe to our biological mother
Who, besides her many rare gifts,
Grants us a tiny biophysical battery
Gulping Oxygen in each cell known as the mitochondrion:
An amazing engine of energy production
Supplying the vital power to cells for our bodily functions

Also, all the mitochondria of this miniature universe
Are solely derived from our biological mothers
Without any input from the father whatsoever
So, we owe all our vital power to our Biological Mother
As maternal mitochondria is the only energy-link
Between the cells in us and the rest of the universe

Again, the mitochondrial DNA is truly discrete
And sited in the mitochondria unlike other DNA matter
So, acting as an extra-nuclear DNA pool
It is only maternal nature manifested in all living creatures

And since a single pool of cosmic power runs this universe,
There is got to be one Cosmic Mother as its sole controller
Whose body must be this incredible making of infinite forms
Held by the vast expanse of Her unique consciousness
In which all conscious creatures like us

Are vital yet very tiny parts of a vast universal network
So, even if naively, we live within this Universal Mother
And She is the One behind the scenes taking care of us!

Hey, children of this ever-wakeful omnipotent mother
No matter where you are
Just feel the power of this blissful reality within yourself
While intensely praying for her
And soon She will join you in your inner heart for sure
Without delaying much further
Since Mother cannot stay aloof when the children want her!
As children are the loving shares of her own burning desire

So, harbor no fear!
Om Mortal Mother Om — Om Immortal Mother Om!!!

--Phoenix, AZ; 2/2/2002

*This poem is dedicated to our beloved Swami Sarvadevananda of
Hollywood Vedanta Society who inspired me to write this during an
intimate conversation on 1/26/2002 in Phoenix, Arizona

Subjective vs. Objective Quest

Almighty God, the creator of this universe
Made us, the humans, in His true reflection,
And things that we perceive and treasure about us
Offer straight testimony to this profound assertion
As gauged by our acute feeling and valued intellect;
The mightiest tools given to us by our Creator

We know from our daily encounter in this universe
That the fundamentals of creative principles truly are
Dedicated feeling, steady intellect and strong desire
That all of us enjoy in our daily exploratory affairs
For grasping any truth that we sincerely desire, but
With ill motifs however we suffer a gloomy disaster

A distilled intellect guided by a deep acute feeling
Is indeed the best innovator we can even imagine
Either in a subjective or an objective investigation
And the truth in both cases is felt as the bliss within
Thus assuring us of reaching the correct destination
With the clearest affirmation with no confusion

Though truth always exist independent of a viewer
Subjectively it is empty if not realized by the viewer
Creating the expansion of a person's consciousness
Or else who would even bother to go after the truth?
So, the joy of gaining insight is the cherished prize
That we instantly harvest from the pursuit of truth.

Truth is scattered around both without and within
Yet feeling for its realization comes firmly from within
And as it gets down to the issue of the ultimate Truth
The entire investigation also undergoes within
And the method used for this is called Meditation
Where progress is gauged by the drop in inner tension,
That turns into blissfulness following its resolution

And the truth so realized is known as the Subjective truth
In contrast to the other method, known as Objective quest
For finding a truth known as the scientific truth
Even though the former is more scientific than the later
Since there is hardly any room for speculation in the former

So, subjective quest is vital for the realization of holistic truth
Whereas the Objective one is good mostly for a partial truth,
But for a healthy joyous living however
Both plans must be harmoniously pursued.

-- Phoenix, AZ; 2/26/02

The Ego Vs. Super-Ego

The usual practice and the process
Through which we get our external message
Is via the action of sense input on brain neurons
Where electric signals are serially transformed
Into neurotransmitters and pituitary hormones
Which in turn does the blood carry
On to the target endocrine glands
For further emission and flow of specific hormones
To act on the specific target tissues
Giving a final metabolic expression of our emotion
And the net outcome of the entire process
Is always dictated by the ego of a person
Since nature of the initial thought-signal
Is normally filtered by his ego prior to final execution

There is another novel process
For prompt processing of all our environmental message
Mediated by the mighty super-Ego that we all posses
Bypassing the traditional thought circuit
And the messages in these cases
Travel straight into the person's heart
Without being altered by his biased ego, and
On such occasion, the person is well-known to cherish
An impartial intellect with acute feeling
Commonly known as the blissful superconsciousness:
A holistic state of wisdom of the being
Engaged in spontaneous action having no ego interjection
Since the being ubiquitous in us acting as the ego
Is reduced to a faint dot desiccated by the distilled intellect
In this tranquil sphere of our balanced inner horizon

-- Phoenix, AZ; 5/29/02

18

The Nature Of Reality
Science Concurs With Spirituality
(Taken From a Fable of Sri Ramakrishna)

"Let me explain the nature of reality**," said Sri Ramakrishna
A self-realized Vedantin and the 19th century Spiritual Giant from
India
Who often compared the temporary human body as an earthen
pitcher, and
Declared that our mind-body pair acts as mirror to realize things in
Nature
"Suppose there are nine earthen pitchers brimmed in water and
are
Reflecting the sun" so he asked, "how many suns would be visible
there?"
"A total of ten sir, nine images and the real sun" was the answer
"One pitcher is now broken, how many suns would then remain?"
"Nine, eight images and one real sun" was the natural answer
"Another is now broken again how many would remain then?"
"Eight, seven images and one real sun" was the obvious answer,
and
Six more were similarly broken and the disciple had right answers
each time
And then came the moment of truth to the last pitcher when
Sri Ramakrishna asked, "Break that one too and tell me the
number again"
"Only one sir, the true sun" was the clear and confident answer,
when
The Master said with a smile "no sir, the reality of the sun itself is
in question here
Since no pitcher is left behind to report on the sun any longer

So, who is to tell about the true sun in the absence of an
observer?"
Thus with so much simplicity he enlightened the nature of reality
That nobody could ever complain about its lack of lucidity
Thus, the nature of reality is phenomenal and a very personal one,
and
Depends on the subjective relation between the object and the
observer
As told in the story above with sun reflected in the pitcher as
metaphor
And each one of us with varying experience creates our own
universe
Thus things are there as they truly are but we see them in ways
they reflect in us!

-- 12/29/2001

*Like Sri Ramakrishna, the Nobel Laureate Physicist Neals Bohr
came to the same conclusion decades later in "Objective Existence of
Phenomenon Independent of Their Means of Observation" stating
that "In the reality that exists 'out there' in the absence of an observer
it is meaningless to ask questions about its nature of reality." Thus like
Sri Ramakrishna, Bohr and Heisenberg maintained that observation
alone constructs reality. Therefor, observership is a prerequisite for a
meaningful version of reality. Hence the old idea of an objective world
is not tenable any longer, following the introduction of Quantum
Mechanics in modern physics.*

The Universal Computer
Science Concurs with Spirituality

This universe is an endless database likened to an endless server
For a vast network of self replicating, self-programming computers
In which a lot have marginal ability compared to the rest
Yet all enjoy intrinsic resource as a way to survive and self-defense

These living computers consist of numerous feedback loops
Totally coupled to one another for the benefit of the whole
Where each loop has its vital role in the grand holistic scheme
So best performance by the individual loop is the only preferred goal

This computer is a whirlpool-construct meant for controlled motion
Sustained by the nonstop flow of thoughts, energy and information
That hold a range of vortex loops with many a frequency of vibration,
Divinely united by Mother Nature for proper wellness of the whole

It is the consciousness part of this living computer that is only real
Being forever changeless, it truly is as it was in time immemorial
And, by its unique ability in feedback control it channels power to all
The paraphernalia wrongly think however, they own the power within

So, consciousness is the ultimate reality in this vast elusive universe;
Where it, being the organizing power, is the life force of these computers
And, truth about this grand unity can be known by a supposed owner
By melting own limited consciousness into the vast ocean of this universe!

--Tempe, Arizona 85210, 8/9/2003

21

Appearance

Please show me now your catholic heart
And take my heart in your sight
And fill the gruesome void of my mind
With spontaneous joy of your light

Not being aware of the truth in your making
With so much skill that you designed,
I took them for real only on face value
Without a clue, that you're eternally behind

But now I know in the heart of my heart
That you alone are the truth, and
As consciousness alone you linger behind all
So, the names and forms are untrue.

I was raised to trust only this world of forms
Which too I do now by habit
As my habit mind tricks me like a magic-spell
Moving too fast for me to check it

So much is my misery from pain as a result
(Oh dear) I can't take it any longer
Please let me feel you in person right now
Please come to my longing heart chamber!

Written originally in Bengali on 5/18/1988 (subsequently published in my book, Ek Peyelar Jannya; Academic Press, Calcutta in 1996), andTranslated into English in its final form on 4/15/2000; Phoenix, Arizona

OM Poems II:

On Devotion

Christmas Prayer

On this day of Christmas
We kneel before Thee oh my Lord
The Lord of the Universe
Who appears on earth in human forms
Like Krishna, Buddha, Moses and Jesus
And so many other enlightened teachers
That this World has ever seen
Since the dawn of human civilization

Oh dear Lord
Please let us not forget
That you are the beginning and the end
And not any of your enlightened children
That the holy men are only the means to your end
Since they too found an end in yourself
And You became the center of their whole being
As their thoughts, words and deeds reveal
Hence, we must try to feel their feelings
By joining own hearts to those of the holy men
And thus in essence try to be their being!
This is indeed the spirit of their great teaching!

Oh, my undying universal consciousness
The nearest of all our nears
You are the center of our living universe.
And occupying the very core of our heart
You preside over our mind in numerous desires
And thus play your eternal games with us, where
We too with own wills play individual parts.

Oh Lord please guide us to play our parts right
Like those of the well-known mystic players
Including our merciful Avatar, beloved Jesus,
Who died as a model for us on the holy Cross-!

-- Phoenix, AZ; 12/25/2001

Friendly Father

Oh universal Father, our invisible friend
Living in the grandeur of your own creation
You are forever playful and bereft of any frustration
That incites in us so much wonder
Why do your children like us suffer so much?
Where have we gone wrong?

You are forever gloriously beautiful
Like youthful children, blooming flowers and pure nature
Always pristine and peaceful
Spanning this vast Universe among the singing stars
Forever enjoying anew and afresh
Your abundant creations in spontaneous bliss
Becoming of yourself this incredible universe
From your eternal consciousness that also made us conscious

So, we too are part of the same undying reality as you are
Yet, owing to ignorance we suffer
As we are too scared to part with our material nature
Thinking that this material body is our only self, thus suffer

In reality You and I have been together through eternity
Over this endless time and space
While you opted to separate yourself from us to play
Giving us this mind, body and Free Will for creative display
And instead, we willed a shield of selfish ego
Distancing you further from us
Thus sustaining this ongoing suffering in us
While your play is meant for fun alone and none else

Thus, the ignorant humans like us
Lead a life of unconscious, like a lesser animal
Being unconscious of our own blissful consciousness
Hence being oblivious of who we really are
We go through this debacle in life
Building better cocoons to isolate us even further
But alas!
If we a had chance to feel Thy glowing presence in us!
Only for once!
Oh Heavenly Father, our eternal benevolent friend
Please help awakening us!

-- Phoenix, AZ; 6/6/2002

Gold Ornaments

I am not eager for Thy golden decors,
But keen for its essence alone --
The innate quality that makes the gold golden,
Making it appealing to all the human

It's not much fun to possess your gold
Since it draws jealousy from others
As seen by myself and told by many folks,
And warned by the great yogi masters

The possession of gold inflates my ego,
Which make me suffer in turn
Which is why I abhor your material gold
But have my heart golden in return.

If you please do care to grant my desire,
With your unique golden favor;
With instant effect I would stain my ego,
And serve the mankind with pleasure.

Please do destroy all my material charms,
From the very core of my heart;
And make me focused to their intrinsic values
In order to quench my thirst

-- Phoenix, AZ 85008

In Communion With my Mother

Never did I want to bind you, but desired
To love you deeply with my heart and soul,
To feel you acutely in all facets of my life, and
To find my true self in the mirror of your soul

With such a keen desire, oh mother I was
Connected to your soul the world over,
Along the longest path of my lone journey
While you orchestrated a melodious tune
With this tender flute of yours

Today, you live no longer, oh mother
In that familiar temple of your mortal body
Where you played for decades the games of life
With a compassionate heart and a masterful mind

Yet I get to feel that familiar feeling in my heart,
Through the power of your undying love for me,
As, you became an adorable shining star
In the divine sky of my inner sanctuary

Wrote in Bengali on 2/11/97 in Salt Lake, Calcutta (India) the day after the demise of my beloved mother and published in 1996 in "Ek Peyelar Janna" (Academic Press, India). Translated into English on 2/11/99

Jesus Christ on the Cross

Behold our beloved Jesus bleeding on the holy Cross-
The embodiment of pure love in deep compassion
His huge heart embraces all through relentless love
Even though his body suffers from the dreadful pain

Smilingly does he endure pain to get his point out
That love, as the reality of our soul is deathless
And the only function of our brief mind-body outfit
Is to give a face to love through bodily emotion
So, the unseen light of our heart could be seen
And the magic of selfless love could be felt within

So, to follow the path of Jesus is to follow his loving heart
And be totally keen in tuning in to His great Eternal Soul
Which He did reveal so vividly in His very last moments
By rejecting own earthly body like a broken earthen bowl

This precious undying love of Jesus is available to all
Which a genuine seeker of the end Truth can verify within
Upon joining own heart to that of our Lord on the Cross, and
Opening it, as He did, to the consciousness of the universe
Then live in a state of enduring bliss as long as we live
Using this gift of Christ-love for the good of all creatures!

-- Tempe, AZ 85281; 10/7/03

31

Long Wait

Oh my beloved, where are you?
It seems like the eternity,
That I have been waiting
And waiting keenly to be at your service
With all your chosen necessities,
Carefully selected and held
In my lonely little home
Oh, please come!

I have been waiting and waiting,
With all panes of my home, widely open,
And all my rooms fully festooned;
But alas, all have been turned into vain!

Time and again you have tested me
All life long, oh my dear,
Only to prepare me for this turbulent world
Bit by bit only stronger!
But, please don't let me have to wait
In this manner any longer!
Since I can't bear this sort of being,
This life of endless waiting any more!

I am sure that you shall come,
When the time is right, and ripe for me.
So, I didn't mind to wait this long
With my longing heart glued to your path.
But now I feel I am ready for you, my beloved
Please don't make me wait much longer.

Please give me endless patience, and
Don't ever let frustrations come upon me
This is my only prayer, my dear
That I pray day and night before Thy altar.

I do want to partake in your game
And this profound desire alone
Has kept me going all this long
So please fulfill my desire soon
By allowing me to have a good feel
Of your fun-filled, eternal game!

-- 4/15/1987

Lord Krishna
(In The Battle of Kurukhetra)

Behold our beloved Krishna in the bustle of the battlefield
The essence of all human virtue as the supreme Godhead
As the charioteer of Arjuna amid muddle of the war-drums
Counseling his worried friend on the nature of the battle of Dharma

Bhagbat Geeta is the telling of the Lord to war-anxious Arjuna
And the essence of this version is now all too well known
That led Arjuna to fight firm and win the battle in the end
Showing a strong mental uplift that anyone could go along

Work must we always perform according to our innate nature
As none can flee from work, yet fulfill ones heart's desire
So our duty is to find a path based on the balanced ethics
And stay on the fair mode in our thoughts, words and deeds

Like a Karma-Yogi should we act with command over own mind
With a heart full of compassion and a feel for everyone around
So objective actions could be taken in the interest of all concerned
And harmony could be made certain in the minds of all around

The best way to perform work is to work for the sake of work
With no anticipation whatsoever on the fruits of the works done
Except for a joyous privilege of giving one's best in the action
Leaving the fruits to the Indweller Lord for avoiding all reactions

Karma must we all do according to our personal Dharma
And should do it in a selfless mode for the benefit of all in mind
Only then would we be able to pass the bad effects of Karma
Preserving our inner peace by the grace of Lord Krishna

-- 10/15/2003, Tempe, AZ 85281

34

Mindfulness

Oh my anonymous omnipresent poet
The conductor of this great world band
You are the father of all possible music
And mother of all scenes, petite or grand

Sitting at the core of my innermost heart
Beyond the reaches of my senses
You are always busy playing own music
To appease my body and my senses

So long I was ignorant of this simple fact
That you are the player behind my flute
I was worried, baffled and sad, all that
And shy due to clumsiness with my flute

But now I'm certain that I'm the top hand
As you are the conductor of my game
I have only to join you and play my role
And have fun in playing the same.

-- Phoenix, AZ 85008; 9/30/02

OM Mother OM: Our Eternal Beloved

Behind this obvious panoramic universe
Lays its mystery and deep-seated cause:
The cause of all causes
But it's neither visible nor intelligible to us
Since it's too subtle and too novel
That our faulty intellect fails to relate:
It is an ocean of energy carrying waves of joy
The joy of ever-new creativity and vision
Gushing out of a tide of overflowing love that is
Love bubbling over for the sake of love alone
Here Love herself embody all creation and beauty

She's our dancing universe – the dancing queen
Forever lost in her self-absorbing rhythm
She's singing universe too – the singing queen
Where the singer and her song lost all distinction
Also, She's the eternal poet
Where the poet embody all articulation of her poems
From the past, the present and the time yet to come

All her thoughts are laced to one universal rhythm
Her all-pervading "A-U-M" is her primordial song
All her lexis keeps making her ever-new poems
Forever singular she is and beyond all comparison

She is the self-luminous Consciousness Herself
Encased in a cosmic body of incessant creation
And as the creator and sustainer of all
She's not only the source, she is way much more
She's the Mother of this Universe
Just a glance from whom alone
Could make us perceive things utterly clear
Making a mortal life harmonious and wholesome

She is our very own compassionate Mother
And forever staying behind our egoistic minds
She is the One taking care of all our wants
So, let us take refuse in her together, and
Feel her countless blessings for now and forever
Remaining ever indebted and ever intoned
"OM Mother OM!"

-- Phoenix, AZ; 2/5/2002

My Little Violin

Oh my Beloved, please teach me,
Please teach me how
To play this little violin of mine;
Then allow me to join
In your incredible timeless orchestra

I am awfully anxious,
To play in your game,
But don't know how!
Being unskilled in the art
And unable to partake
All my day and night I cry
In pain and agony
Oh my beloved, teach me
Please teach me how!

My little violin is my only means
To share your divine joy
Oh dear, I can't bear
This separation of hearts
No more, no more!
Oh please, my Beloved,
Please teach me how
By holding my unskilled hands
Please enable them to join you
In your eternal orchestra!

Oh my Beloved,
You are the heart of my heart --
I owe you everything I have got
Even my very own soul;
So, must you teach me how!
But, please my beloved,
Please do hurry!
I can't bear to wait any more,
Not any more!!

Written originally in Bengali on 11/21/1987 (subsequently published in my book, Ek Peyelar Jannya; Academic Press, Calcutta in 1996), and Translated into English in its final form on 2/18/2000; Phoenix, Arizona

Poetic Connection

Oh, indeed I do not write my poems
They happen to come to my pen
And flow across to express my thoughts
As long as the feelings remain

Spontaneously they come
And spontaneously they go
Independent of my time and space
I only seize the moment in deep contemplation
And let words flow at its pace

The thoughts I cherish
In my deep-seated mind
Often hide in a submerged land
And flow on its own in the form of a poem
Like a breeze in a dream island

The joy that trails
Forms a stream of bliss
Where I take a dive for fun, and
Stay there alone to enjoy the moments
For as long as I can

It's the Mind of the Universe
Just working through me
That I know for sure, and
I'm only a tool in the hands of my Beloved
Like a wave of the ocean, nothing more!

-- Phoenix, AZ 85008; 10/21/2001

Sri Guru OM

OM, Sri Guru OM!
You have come to be the Kohinoor of my crown
That helps me feel your glowing presence
As a reminder of yourself, as the transcendental self
So, you're the only source of my love and wisdom.

And I adore you on the same lofty chair
As my beloved father and mother
As mere thought of you brings joy in my heart
And blessed I feel by your transcending look.

Now I feel by your divine grace
That forever you lead me holding my hand
Giving me solace in times of doubt
With your radiant light in my heart and mind

You pick me up often as soon as I fall
And remove the web of Maya in front of me
Giving me warning prior to any pitfall
So, I may be saved from future pains.

Forever you appear in human forms
To offer wisdom to the needy souls
So needless suffering can be shunned or reduced
And ignorant souls have a chance to be redeemed.

Oh Gurudeva,
What else could I say about yourself?
I love you as much as I love my very own self
Since a simple thought of you

Makes me dwell in my innermost heart
As a mere speck in Thy all-inclusive self
Shining steadily in that serene realm
OM Sri Guru OM

Written originally in Bengali on 6/30/1988 (subsequently published in my book, Ek Peyelar Jannya; Academic Press, Calcutta in 1996), and Translated into English in its final form on 4/15/1997; Phoenix, Arizona

Sri Ramakrishna
(1836 – 1886)

Lo and behold our Unity-Avatar, Jagat-Guru Sri Ramakrishna
The incarnation of highest love that is called *Prema*
Being poised in *Sukhasana* for the universe to learn
That Prema is the only way to attain the highest individual Dharma

The Lord's body is radiating Prema like that of a playful child
The endless source of this pure love is His chaste holistic consciousness
Which he emits in ceaseless bliss through every pore of his body
Our master's way of showing the world how to conclude ones Karma

The Lord is hereby showing the world what he cherished in life
That Prema is the only way for a man to get hold of the whole Truth
That all other means might take one only close to her inner God
But never close enough to feeling Him both within and without

Our Lord was always coupled to God in thoughts, words and deeds
As was revealed with total sureness to all his nearest devotees:
That mind-body outfit was only his tool to direct his priceless Prema
Emitting steadily from the Lord's being to all those around him

The entire life of our beloved Lord is his open teaching to all
Faithfully recorded by his able disciple, best known as Sri-M
With great precision in Lord's version in the Gospels of Sri Ramakrishna
Serving thereafter as a genuine guide through this baffling world realm

-- Tempe, AZ 85281; 10/29/2003

The Great Meditating Buddha

Behold the splendor of Lord Buddha immersed in deep meditation!
His heart's compassion happens to encompass all living soul
His divine tongue seems busy in relishing the bliss within
His third eye seems excelling the Truth in an all-absorbing vision
His sharp intellect is shining steady like the divine glory of the Sun!
So attaining the whole Truth within
The Lord has become at one, and
Becoming the Light unto Himself right now
He has attained the end in blissful unity
At the endless source of the universal saga of fun!

-- Tempe, AZ; 10/2/2003

Who Am I?

Eternal consciousness is what you are
Oh Mother (or Father), and
Bliss is your primordial nature
So, this is what I came to realize in the end
That from bliss I came, by bliss I am sustained
And into bliss I enter again
So, Truth-Consciousness-Bliss or *Sat-Chit-Anandam*
Is what I really am!

So, my beloved Mother, you and I are truly the same!
Where you are the totality and I am your tiny fraction
But none the less, one and the same
Like a drop of rain in the limitless ocean
Where I am within you
And you are all over me
But without this stubborn "me", Oh Mother
You have no game!

This is why you devised this mind-body machine
To make the appearance of an apparent partition
Just to play your illusory games
With this ignorant son of yours:
This self-organizing, self-rectifying ego machine
And show me clearly at the very end
My deathless self again removing all my ignorance
Thus, helping me feel your endless bliss
In my deepest inner silence!

So, my beloved Mother, here I am,
Living heartily in your Sat-Chit-Ananda ocean
Always immersed in your holy name
Knowing that bountiful diversity in our virtual universe
Is owing to your own primordial power
That supports all conscious creatures like us
And is only conceived by your own Supreme Intelligence,
Oh my omnipresent all-powerful Mother,
To fulfill your innocent desires in your caring universe!

Very truly yours,
This mortally immortal, "Me"!

-- Phoenix, Arizona; 9/19/2002, in final form on 7/2/2003

OM Poems III:

On Self-Knowledge

A Gift of Love

In that peaceful multihued fall evening
Just in time for my daily meditation
A bird song loomed near out of nowhere
In my mental space claiming my attention
And traveled straight into my inner heart
Without seeking any formal permission:
My self was quick to recognize it
At the same instant, and
Melted in her musical note as they met

I was busy in my consciousness workout
When that happened
About to dive to my deeper self
As the experience goes
Making an effort to melt my mind
In my whole body feeling
Like a nestled bird fostering her eggs
To fetch her unborn

My mind soon moved into my throat
Close to my tongue
As the nectar of bird song began flowing free
For myself to taste
Then the Yoga between the bird and myself
Was fully done
As I remained tuned to her drunken soul
Joined with mine

Music and the musician are inseparable
They all say
As music flows from the deepest core
Of a devout singer
Yet my soul can feel that old bird-song
Past so many days even now
Since a gift of unconditional love
Is in fact, mysterious like that
Somehow!

-- 2/6/96

Beloved

Oh my omnipresent beloved,
With sheer joy, I came to realize in the end
That scheming my body by your divine will
You have desired to dwell within
Sharing my fun loving heart, and
Playing games with my imperfect intellect
So as to reveal to me my true nature at last!

Larger than the universe you are, and
Smaller than the smallest I am
Yet, you trust me with a role in so vital a game
That thrills me in joy as I begin to act
That I am here to live your delightful ideals
In my daily living part

So, my beloved, here I am
To join you with my fervent soul
In your eternal game
With a purpose and a goal
To serve you by my mortal body and immortal soul
And dedicate my life for such a purpose
Perceiving you in every being living around us

Oh my beloved, dearest of my dear
This is my sole desire, that
The information you granted me I want to share
With the rest of humanity
That in reality we indeed are
An integral part of your vast Conscious reality
Hence, the same as your blissful immortality,

Thus, being fully aware
Of our divinity, potential and true nature
We must be able to chart the right courses
And make the most of our individual talents,
Thus could indeed make us in the end
Truly creative and blissfully prosperous!

-- 3/24/01

Biofeedback In Yoga Asanas

Feedback Control is a mighty device:
A perceptive supple system inherited by all
For self-rectification at the psychophysical plane,
Letting us maintain our inner balance,
And providing the needed skills for self-composure
Yet, most of us are unaware of this awesome power.

Feedback is a divine system in us that deals with
Our body movement, intellect and acute feeling
That we encounter during the alert *Yoga Postures*
When feeling and intellect unite to amalgamate,
To form an unity among the mind, body and soul
Only then do we realize the art of feedback control
And how flawlessly holistic this power really is!

Under the astute conditions of *Yoga Asanas*,
Feedback feeling stays alert to gain information
About our mind-body integration
Without intrusions from the random thoughts
In full cooperation with our distilled intellect
While making the needed correction
Using acute feeling as the sole guide for inner control,
Thus leading us gently to the desired holistic goal
For the ultimate unity in our mind, body and soul
When pure joy softly suffuse our whole consciousness
Assuring us that we have truly reached the goal
And that's how precise this subjective *yoga science* is
In dealing with our innate feedback control!

-- Phoenix, AZ 85008; 10/1/2002

53

Escaping the Net: The End of Illusion

Who wants to be trapped in this wide enchanting net?
That has been cast so cleverly over the cosmos?
It brings us pain time and again
Yet neither can we stop it from happening.
We feel powerless in controlling our desires and urges
Which compel us to desire things all the more

And it's not the end if a desire is fulfilled just once
Since it only inflames our desire for more passions.
Thus, continues our stride without an end in sight
Looking for more sensations as the time goes on.
If for any reason a desire goes unrealized
It stays as a sorrow until becomes realized
So, this becomes a two-way sword indeed, and
As far as the anguish goes there seems to be no end.

Thus, all material delights are no more than illusion
Since happiness does not reside inside any matter
But acting as attractors by the power of our desires
They make us intent for more and more delusion

Hence, question has been asked
Time and time again in the past
Is there a way out of this whirlpool of mess?
And according to the wise, yes there is
One, and only one such way
And it works without fail they do forcefully say
But there is a price that one must be willing to pay.

But no price can be big enough for a lasting peace
Since that is what all of us are really after
But keeps on looking wrongly in material things,
And the wise tells us so with an assured face.

The wise have been telling us time and again
That all attempts to douse flames with inflammables
Are bound to be disastrous and end up in vain.

Solution then lays in controling the mind:
This is certainly not an easy thing to act
But it is doable since many has walked this path
So one has to proceed by taking comfort in that

The wise say thus, we must change ourselves first
Ahead of any crazy ideas of changing others
And this has got to be our primary focus
Because the problem lays only within us
As our conditioned mind makes us run so wild
And the wise have all along been telling us that.

Problem rests in the wrong identification of us,
And the wrong way of using our valued intellects
Creating wrong habits, bad karma and wrong desires
That really put us into such an incredible mess.

Yet as pure consciousness, we are the ultimate truth
That transcends all boundaries of material nature, and
Mind, body, intellect are part of that grand architecture
That fool us believing other than what we really are
Because our senses are set with very limited power
Making the mind think our body is what we are

Thus the path of yoga is the path to follow, and
And discover our true self as the Spirit at last,
Then start enjoying life in all its waking hours
As a detached free soul in this enchanting universe.

The journey ends in the spirit nature in the long run
By realizing own individual soul as the end goal
When the charm of Maya fails to enchant any longer
As he sees his own soul dwelling everywhere
Hence becoming an end to his own true soul
A man turns his life on earth as an endless saga of fun

-- 5/14/2001

Life Cycle

Life is a time-bound training plan for all human soul
And death is an end to one of many such journeys
While Astral-world is an interim space for self-appraisal
Pending to get right parents for rebirth of an eager soul

Thus returns the soul on earth time and again
To fulfill many desires that it happens to hold
Until securing own divinity while serving on earth
When the cycle of birth and death ceases to an end

Then that free soul becomes an end in itself
Being one with the infinity as an ever blissful soul
And chooses to live along as a grand universal self
For the benefit of humanity as it's only loving goal

-- 5/25/2003

Living with God Within*

Things are there as they truly are
But we see them simply by the color of our mind
And make all judgments for good or bad
By reacting naively with our conditioned mind

Thus, we fail to see the plan of God
Behind the glamour of His unparalleled creation
As we dwell on the exterior of the things we desire
Ignoring our links with the core of all desirable things

Let's learn to act from the feeling of own heart
Where things do shine as in a clean mirror
And learn to play from that center around
When mind stays cool in its original ground
Dwelling peacefully in its spiritual nature
And lives with a sense of stillness within

Then the essence of all things external to us
Is perceived profoundly by our Soul within
When mind and body become friendly to us
As our journey towards God thus truly begins

Then, we feel within us a fountain of bliss
As our mind-body pair obeys the spiritual nature
When consciousness alone stands as the "I-within"
Being one in "consciousness of the vast Universe"

This "all-pervading-I" is the God within us
Where we feels as a focus of this blissful power
Hence the purpose of our life is to realize just that
And live in that modality for now and forever

So the surest way to commune with our God
Is to get our senses first melted in the intellect;
And melt intellect in turn into our "I-consciousness,"
Then becoming a part of the "vast God-consciousness"
Just hangout as a "droplet" in His oceanic Universe

-- Phoenix, Arizona; 2/19/2002

*This Vedantic science of self-discovery has been taught by numerous self-realized souls in India from the prehistoric times, and is the most scientific and thoroughly walked path hitherto known to mankind for experiencing God (or the ultimate reality) within oneself.

Love OM

Love is an amazing thing
That stays beyond our scheming mind
Being too unique for most to comprehend
It defies all the laws of worldly dealings

Yet, love is so easy to feel within
For, love is fulfillment
Love is surrender
Love is both and yet surpasses both
Love is attachment
Love is detachment
Love is both and yet transcends both
Love is freedom in action
Love is freedom from action
Love is spontaneity without reaction

Love embodies all yet rises above all
Love is freedom of self
Love is freedom from self
Love is personal and impersonal as well
Love is our self-regulating totality
The all-pervading unity
And at once infinitesimal and infinity

Love is the essence of all existence
And the last invisible matrix of this vast cosmos
That only creates and recreates for own glory.
And, as a powerful account of our almighty spirit
Love playfully acts with our narrow intellect
To help us craft our own destiny
While hiding behind our free Will all along

To feel selfless love is to be aware of our divinity
And to be a playful soul lost in love within
Is a very real experience of that deathless reality
In the midst of all our mortal identity
So, even though nearest to our holistic feeling
Selfless love is far from our egocentric intellect

Accordingly, oh my darling mind
Abandoning all efforts to comprehend love
Just surrender your ego to Love within
Then love will reward you in most abundance
Revealing, you and love as one and the same
As you become an end in yourself in the end
Attaining the highest blissful reality
That you have ever been able to comprehend
AUM! Love AUM!

-- 2/20/2002

Me and My Home

This virtual Universe I reflect upon
Is my spiritual home
As, I take great pleasure in roving in her
As my sole travel mate
So, it's only odd to have any sort of fear
In here for me anymore
Since myself and my soul-mate Universe
Have truly become one

These atoms and molecules
Of this brief body of mine
Are parts of the same pool of matter
Of this passing universe at large
But due to my unique soul consciousness
That I have been blessed to possess
By virtue of Her divine grace
I can feel the thrill of Her symphony
In and around me

I do feel now in my heart and soul, that
Many a lives I had lived in this wonderland:
My home of grand charm in many past calls,
To enjoy Her novel splendors in numerous forms
From many a shelters in Her catholic Self
And drank Her peerless bliss
Time and time again
With this divine Soul mate of mine
Cuddled to my whole being

-- 3/11/2001

The Little Boat

In our sense-bound world driven by desires
Covered by many a slippery paths
It's awfully easy to slip into the errors, and
Suffer from them as a consequence
So wake up my friends and
Get hold of your own little boat
Likely to lose control at any moment

In many turns of this twisted journey
Distractions are hiding in disguise
And fed by the habit-mind they thrive.
If we could keep our intellects alert
And hold mind focused on our goal
The distractions will loose all power
In casting their spells on us for sure

Another skill is a must for a soft landing
That all acts must precede careful thoughts
Paying due attention to the pros and cons
With a fearless heart and a steady mind

It must be clear to the mind without fail
That our heart's desire is to reach the goal
And such mind will never fail to be faithful
So, we need not be afraid of it any more

The sail-wind is already here my friend
Just get hold of your rudder secured now and
Sail your boat with single-minded devotion
And no doubt, you'll reach the correct destination!

Written originally in Bengali on 10/28/1987 (subsequently publishedin my book, Ek Peyelar Jannya; Academic Press, Calcutta, 1996), and Translated into English on 3/20/1998

The Self

The milky white blossoms in my little Ivey grove
Went off dancing in the sodden west wind, and
Cheered up my morning in the cloud-breaking sun
While swamping my garden with an unsaid tune

Their lyric wasn't meant to be an audible one
But its sense became so clear to me,
That a phrasing wasn't felt even that necessary
Whatever might that be!
But it indeed was for the passion of their life
I could certainly tell
It was a dance of the deepest inner joy
A celebration of the innermost self!

When a self does connect to another keen self
Words become redundant there
Then the essential truth just promptly pops out
And things become suddenly clear!
Communion really is the name of communication
When it comes down to self
Our senses do not make then any more sense
Neither the intellect seems to be of any big help!

-- 3/7/2001

Towards Noble Desires

Adult souls are at times busy with a certain tug of war
Among gratification of his own ego and own ethical role
And typically in most cases they feel a strong pull
Toward own usual affinity for a self-indulgent goal

So the challenge to a person is to find inner poise
And stay at the center with a steady alert mind
Guarding herself keenly against any troubling urge
And focussing to the overall good never looking behind

Often, our very first thought is a true feedback guide
That spontaneously appears as a signal in the heart
Thereby, listening to the spirit only instead of our mind
A true balance could be reached in a real short time

Meditation is a great way to find a poised mind
By tuning into own center and communing with the soul
Then watching own thoughts and bent of the mind
We could encode it correctly and tilt to the right goal

Hallmark of a good desire is the maintenance of poise
When the decision is made with the totality in mind
Having a win-win condition for all the parties concerned
The basic inequity in the issue is correctly addressed.

-- Tempe; 11/21/03

OM Poems IV:

On Holistic Truth

Art of Living

Let's not allow our ego to overvalue ourselves
So, we won't suffer a fall, and
Let's remember not to ever undervalue ourselves
So, we won't degrade own souls

Let's strike a balance between head and the heart
Staying at the Chakra in our throat
When, we can feel the work we are engaged in
And live in the moment as we go

Let us try to be just in everything we do
In thoughts, words and deeds
By embracing the truth with a joyous heart
Let's live within the means in our needs

Nothing could hurt or bother us then
As our intellect will shine only steady
Nor would we suffer from any more reaction,
Or miss any option, as we've always been ready.

-- 5/15/03

Battle Within

In this battle field of life filled with calamity
We often hear the cry of suffering humanity
Here, the words of wisdom are frequently ignored
And the swords of intellect often remain unused

Hey brother, what are you afraid of?
Just jump to the center with your open sword
And destroy all negations blurring your vision
Summoning your courage and hidden compassion

Let the fire of battlefield engulf and burn out
All our junky thoughts making us weak
Then following the inferno we shall find
Only pure love and sure hopes are gleaming behind

We shall see at last the dawn breaking out
With all its magical power in glory
And the cool breeze of love of our universe
Helping us to sail safe among all outer fury

Hey brother, ignorance is our sole enemy
And the only cause of all our plights
So must we keep our sword of intellect shiny
And never let them hide from our sights

*Written originally in Bengali, "Jiban Juddha", on 9/16/1988
(subsequently published in my book, Ek Peyelar Jannya; Academic
Press, Calcutta, in 1996), and Translated into English on 1/12/
1998*

Desire

Last morning,
The bushes of oleanders in my open front-yard
Were found to be bland lacking blossoms
And this morning,
I saw them cheerful in pleasant wonder
They are bejeweled with charming oleanders!

Happily sleeping they had been
In loving bosom of their bushes
And woke up suddenly in clean utter joy
In dancing monsoon showers

Could desire of the buds for self-expression
Had made them blossom here?
Or desires of the plants for self-fulfillment
Had made them come to appear?

While both appear to be the apparent truths
But something else is there
That the related gifts of the monsoon rain
Must have the strong say in here

The whole show is tied to this ONE truth though
Any way we do want to see
That the Universe is really the ultimate authority
Whatever they may seem to be

It's the desire of the Universe in the very long run
That only appears to matter
As all sort of support only come from this resource
No matter how do they seem to occur

-- 3/10/1996

71

Eternity

Another dawn creeps in as the world turns
Another night melts down in a joyous daylight
Here in I watch again the game of my Eternity:
The limitless 'I' in search of Her own limits

Her golden flag does unfold in my eastern sky
That resonates in the music of her march
And permeates all terrains that come to appear
Over her open path covering the endless space

Why does she retrace the path in her daily journey
Time and time again in a cyclic manner forever?
Who else could tell but her?
My all-knowing Eternity?
Perhaps it's her way to relive her creation anew
For the renewal of her saga of fun!

There is an analogy coming to my mind
Which is an experience common to all
Where Eternity is likened to a biological mother
Playing peek-a-boo with her own children!

That is all that ever could be said about Her
Everything else has to be felt in own heart.
Intellect is helpless when it comes to knowing Her,
Since Herself is the creator of this intellect of ours.

She is our consciousness, the supreme monarch
Sole creative power behind this limitless universe
Including this transient body of ours,
And selecting our heartland as her virtual throne
She plays with our narrow intellect
Over and over again, for the sake of endless fun!

-- 3/10/2001

In Search of Peace

Peace is a natural state of every human heart
Waiting to be discovered by the distraught adult soul
Since peace is rooted in the core of our spirit
So to reclaim this peace is our noble spiritual goal

Our spirit is like that of a calm sparkling lake
Where the mind keeps playing on its surface as its surf
So, mind and spirit are truly the same stuff
Only differing fundamentally in their vibratory states

Hence our mind, when fully calm, becomes true-self
Like the waves of a lake, when calm, become the lake
And the surest way to become peaceful in our life
Is to merge into own spirit becoming that lake

We need to be *consciously* conscious of own silly mind
And train it to make it still by controlling our senses
As senses would melt into mind and then into spirit
Enabling us to see all things by our serene spirit divine

To lead a life of harmonious peace is the legacy of a man
By careful cleansing of our impure mind it has to be revived
And, to make our rowdy mind to refrain from sick desires
By directing it to the divine spirit, the basis of all our bliss

-- January 7, 2004

*Mother Earth OM**
Science Concurs With Spirituality

Oh holy Mother Earth, our eternal guardian
The home of all living souls
We owe you everything that we ever stand for
In whatever we cherish and hold.

This body of ours is made from your nature
We live on your water and air
You let us live on the gift of your harvest
As nurtured we are in your care

You display the power of this potent universe:
Revealing the power of your soul
This makes us in turn alert of those spectacles
By virtue of the soul that we hold

Thus, the mother of all mothers is what you are
As we live in your bosom forever
You are the pillar of worldwide consciousness
Which all of us possess and share

We, your children, are demanding in nature
And act from selfish desires
And you, the embodiment of love and patience
Do endure all ailing affairs.

You trust us, granting the power of our will
And crave us to play the honest games
While hiding all along in our innermost heart
You watch us playing the same.

You made the game-rules so plain and simple
Where cause-effects rule all parts
And as long as a person is honest and playful
You shower your bliss in his heart.

Through reward and penalty, we all do learn
How to be happy in this life
And you laugh and cry with your children too
While letting us to do what we like

Your goal is to teach us the truth about reality
Through personal experience of each soul
That your panoramic nature is only an illusion
And to realize your consciousness is our goal.

-- Phoenix, AZ, 9/14/2002

* Consistent with this Yoga Philosophy, the recent scientific GAIA
theory of World Ecology considers the Earth as a vibrant living
organism with numerous feedback control loops to maintain global
health and harmony, and all sentient being including the human are
only part of this vastly complex eco-network

The Purpose of a Human Life

This world is a bountiful creation of a compassionate God
Who wants us to live along with a positive frame of mind
Using own discrimination faculty to the best of our ability
With a curious open mind and a compassionate heart,
While pursuing Dharma and coolly facing the laws of Karma
Always feeling the infinite blessing of God living within us

Thus the purpose of a human life is to feel God's desire
And live a life of inner harmony in our true nature
So, we must know own nature by means of subjective inquests
And follow the personal and social laws needed for own growth

Yoga is the traditional way to gain this subtle knowledge
Using hands-on experience along the well-trodden path
Thus knowing own true nature relative to the universe at large
We do gain right insights to aptly deal with our active universe

Hence, Yoga is the way to bring an unbroken peace in life
Which, in essence, all of us are anxious to gain, but
We must learn Yoga from a proper master in its right mode
For us to gain holistic health in a way that we truly should

-- June 1, 2003; Tempe, Arizona 85281

OM Poems V:

On Thought, Action, Emotion

I Love You

I adore you as a unique creation of God
And love you as the nectar of my soul
No anticipation or bigotry is there, my dear
It is only my desires to love you ever more
Simply out of spontaneity of my inner heart
The same way, I love the bubbly roses
Only for the sake of its own glory --
I love it for its unspoiled beauty --
The beauty for beauty's sake and nothing else

I know there are hundreds of hurdles
On the way to attaining your finest fullness --
Social hurdles, Karmic hurdles and many more
But you got to cross them by fervent endeavor
No easy shortcut is there, my dear
So, go ahead with a focused mind and open heart
And create an enduring inner glow in concert
That would cut through the layers of ignorance
And clear your way.
So, learn to steer this turbulent current of life
Like an expert navigator
Lest, may cost you precious energy and undue delay.

But remember to look out for the quiet wayside,
And find me waiting in patience
To resonate with your pleasure and pains
And taking pride in your overall gains
So, do avoid the irrational ego
That is only self-defeating arrogance
Just banish it and scan the wayside along your way

And see eager me with my treasured garland
Carefully crafted from my life's jewels
Ready to greet you, my darling
Because, I love you always!

Written originally in Bengali on 6/6/1988 (subsequently published in my book, Ek Peyelar Jannya; Academic Press, Calcutta, 1996), and Translated into English on 2/22/1997

Admission of Errors

Nobody can ever grow up committing no errors
As true learning is only gained from the mistakes made
Hence, it is a Natural Law in our changing Universe
That none could ever walk on earth without making errors

It should have been universal in human manners
That none should be afraid of admitting own errors
Yet, why in this world my friend, many of us don't?
And conceal our own errors under a flat timid cover?

Conceding own errors truly expands ones heart
And lightens the soul by lessening the load
So, (oh Mind) don't ever blunder of hiding own errors
Or else, be unable to learn and not grow in the end

Three options are there after committing an error:
To admit to oneself followed by a change in manners
Or reveal to allied parties, assuring not to repeat later
Or ignore it all together, facing the consequence after

Straight confessions always ease a mind off burden
And helps blossoming freely the character of the soul
By making a person first to curtail his own ego
Then teaching him ways to stay calm in the end

So, try to be on the top by prompt admission, oh Mind
Or, wait until you pay a heavy price later, but
Being true to own self by quick confession, my friend
We empower ourselves only to be smarter and better.

*Written originally in Bengali on 9/6/1988 (subsequently published
in my book, Ek Peyelar Jannya; Academic Press, Calcutta, 1996),
and translated into English in its final form on 4/15/2000*

Beauty

Right feeling is critical in the act of beauty enjoyment
Which a beholder has got to master
That he must see the things as they truly are
And not as an objects of own wishful desire
Thus making it clear, beauty is in the eyes of a beholder

A person must at first learn to become a true observer
A fully compassionate and open-minded onlooker, and
See things up from their universal fabric
And see all things as part of a holistic network
Feeling concurrently the joy of creation within
Only then would things reveal their true beauty to us
By inciting a revered feeling of awe and wonder
That will fondly embrace our heart forever
For sharing and caring their full majestic splendor

-- Phoenix, AZ; 1/10/2001

Christmas Greetings

It is that time of the year again
Still filled in the magic spell of fall color
That goes afloat along our life's flow
As part of a train of the eternal rainbow
That keeps on feeding our thirsty souls
In this cosmic panorama of Nature

Our ultimate goal
Is to feel that pulsating soul
All the world over in Mother Nature's lap
And fill our bowl
With the eternal rhythm of life,
That timeless symphony,
Ah!!! The sweetest music of all!

Let the spirit of Christmas
Light up your entire life, and
Shed light with an undiminished glow;
Like the polar star may your everyday life
Be harmonious and peaceful
Whichever way you may choose to go

-- December 2003

Fear

The fear of terror is now running abound
All over the world by terrorist acts
But knowing all facts and how to combat
We must be alert but not panic-struck

Genuine fear is like a good old wine
A bit of which is good for the brain
As it stimulates the nerves and makes us alert
Making ready for action whenever it's deemed

Fear is powered by the might of our thoughts
And that at times get stronger than us
Thus giving undue focus to fearful thoughts
We create a monster that starts controling us

Imaginary fear is like a teen drinking wine
This feeds her heart more than the brain
And helping to build up her more bad emotion
It fuels the fire of her commotion within

The purpose of life is to have fun in action
And of the imagined fear is to spoil all that
Which make us suffer in needless reactions
Too painfully real in our mind and heart

So never let the fear grow in our mind
And never let the fears possess our soul
Thus let's not fall into the trap of the terrorists
And help them achieve their hideous goal

-- Phoenix, AZ 85008; 10/11/2001

For a Lonely Cup

Behold this magic
My cup is just about empty!
Not too long ago, however
It was brimming in potent juicy nectar!

Suddenly it came to my notice
That the nectar was about to vanish
Down the busy path of my edgy journey!
As Life has taken its toll
Due to the discords
Between my body and my soul
As shown by the hallmarks of deep-rooted stress
Creeping out of its secret hiding space,
And are suddenly visible on my ailing bare body
In lines and traces!

Yet, the depth I gained has not been lost in vain
In spite of all the turmoil, agony and pain
I feel something deep down in my heart at last
As part of my lasting gain:
Now I see the Truth holding my feeble bowl
As my innermost beloved, as my eternal Soul,
As I lurk behind the veils of my stress and strain

Now I promise I will
Keep on tending my undying reality
And using persistent Will
Restore fullness in my decaying entities
By aiming healing Prana to those ailing parts
With blessings from my beloved Majesty
Thus, make the most of my weak remains
By making them live again!

Thus in the end I am certain
That, my void will be void-less again
Regaining the spontaneity of my playful soul
For the sake of my cup alone!

Written originally in Bengali on 6/6/1988 (subsequently published in my book, Ek Peyelar Jannya; Academic Press, Calcutta in 1996), and translated into English in its final form on 4/15/2000; Phoenix, Arizona

Goldness

Never did I ask you a thing made of gold
Nor do I honestly care for them
But I do care for your "goldness of gold"
For which awfully hungry I am.
Happiness can never reside in the gold
Neither can it harbor any pain
But selfish ego somehow creeps in my heart
When the gold-stuffs are fetched in.
So, I do crave along for your goldness of gold
That I wish to treasure in my heart
And keep it closely with my tainted mind
Till it becomes the stainless at last!
Also, having the goldness in my possession
I would offer it free to others
So happiness could reign in the heart of all
And my peace may belong to others

-- 3/7/2001

Healing Prayer for Christmas

Dear God, Lord of this Universe
As all-pervading Consciousness your light is reflected in us
Making our material body seemingly consciousness
So, today we decided to pray in this holy temple of our body
And reveal all our troubles that we want you to know
Since blessings for our healings must come from Thee at last

Oh Lord, You are the master Healer
The ultimate Healer of every mind-body on earth
Since, You are the source of all love, energy and intelligence
Manifested all through this infinite Universe
Including the powers of those acting as healers amongst us

Dear Lord, as our true creator,
You are our real Father and not your human forms
So, we urge you on this day to heal us
On this very special day of holy Christmas
Because we have taken refuge in You at last
While thinking about your Avatar son, Jesus
Recollecting his total trust in you and his selfless love for us
While being assured inside that You will certainly heal us.

Now that we know Lord, You heal by Thy Will
All that we need to do now
Is to connect our tiny will with Thy divine Will
And pray for Thy mercy by submitting our ego
Whilst feeling Thy love in us for a radical healing
And healed must we be at last in due course of time

Dear Lord, We, as Thy soon to be awakened children
Wish to have a clear mind in infinite compassion
So, please fill our heart with humility and true vision
And keep our hands engaged in helping the needy
In order to lift some of their painful burden
With the realization that privilege will always be ours
In heartfelt thanks and profound compassion
Hey Men!

-- December 16, 2002

I Will Be

I will be what I will to be–
This is my Song of this day
I am a child of almighty God
So, nothing can stand on my way

I feel His power in all my senses
In thoughts, words and deeds
I only live as a child of my beloved
Who meets all of my needs

Rich I am by virtue of His power
He is the source of my bliss
It is His love that holds me steady
So, I will be what I will to be

-- June 23, 2003

Illusory World

Discriminate the truth from untruth
And stick on to the truth boldly
Then your contradiction is bound to be gone soon,
Oh Mind, if you could hold on to the truth strongly

The truth personified is like the sun my friend,
Revealing the things as they are
Only the veils on our mind distort the reality,
Making our visions to blur

The desert-mirage allures the traveler,
Who craves to quench his thirst -
It is his desire alone that triggers the illusion,
With untamed passion in his heart

When a trekker sees the truth in a mirage,
Using his power of discrimination
He promptly realizes the nature of illusion, and
Proceed calmly towards his destination

Our thoughts to enjoy the things around us
Are prompted by the hidden desire, and
Lack of discrimination on the part of our own
Make them an unhappy affair

Oh my precious Mind --
Please avoid all rushing or running after things
Using your power of discrimination,
If you wish to be free in this life, my friend
From undue sufferings and needless frustrations!

Written originally in Bengali on 10/28/87 (subsequently published in my book, Ek Peyelar Jannya; Academic Press, Calcutta, in 1996), and translated into English in its final form on 4/15/2000; Phoenix, Arizona

Judgment

In this busy world of virtual truth among multitude
Had I been offered the job of a judge
I would have urged Thou to rush wisdom into my heart
So, I could speak the holistic truth at large

Since all of us live under the spell of Maya
And wish to play outwardly rather than in depth
Where genuine bliss is certain to be found within
Yet, most people ignore it without even looking

Often we use our intellect without using the heart
Thus, oblivious of the totality we deal with the scrap
With partial vision later we suffer in delusion
And feeling severed from this world we fall into gloom

Past many a ego trips at last we moan in frustration
Being lost in our jumbled life as to what to do, and
Being all the more helpless by the dark veil of ignorance
The rays of most hopes remain covered by the gloom

Yet source of all power lays in our heart, hey brother
Just take a deep plunge and see it straight
And taking the intellect along while making that trip
You shall see the reality at last gleaming in your heart

Our intellect will shine steady all hours then
With supports from our spirit-self living in the heart
As dark veils from our mind will vanish all together
Chasing away the murky evils impeding our thought

So, I can be a judge though based on the condition
That must Thou hold curative measure in own hands
And I shall only speak out for the humanity to learn
That all of us hold the keys for our own salvation

Phoenix, AZ 85008, 11/12/2002; translated from the original Bengali poem, BICHARAK (published in the book, Ek Peyelar Janna, by Tushar K. Ray in 1996)

Living

The art of living is to love and live
To love and live with our whole being
And to feel in us as we go making deals
By living each act with hope and zeal
Deep in a person rests the true feeling
And feeling in action alone makes true living
When living and loving become one and the same

But as a matter of fact
There is more to our living act than that
Thus people got to judge and discriminate too
Since that is a vital part of the living act
But thinking by itself alone cannot be a living:
For it's only a prelude for the living act
Like making a bed preparing to take a nap:
It is vital in planning state but not a living act

Thinking is a part of our own great intellect
That helps to organize our scattered thoughts
And helps to discern the right from the wrong
Thus preparing the ground for a living act
When feeling does take over as the vital part
So, love can gain power in focused feeling
And help life growing rich in endless living

--10/1/2001

Mistake

Mistakes are the missteps we make along our life's way
But is a healthy thing to happen to any man
As they show rooms in us for our self-improvement
And learning must go on, since to err is only human.

From the mistakes we make we have a lot to learn
Since mistakes can help in crafting our future
When a learner comes clean following an incidence
And becomes real keen to correct own errors
Then past mistakes reveal to him as in a clean mirror
His rooms for self-improvement and needed care;
Only then, can we reach a level of desired perfection
And feel fulfilled in time in our preferred mission.

Satisfaction is gained only by ones honest efforts
And past mistakes can make a man strong in mindset
Until one gains the degree of a desired perfection, and
Experience the bliss of completion in preferred mission.

Life teaches us all by the punishments and rewards
Where acts of mistakes set off the correct feedback
When due care is assured against repeating such errors
Lest one may have to pay too much price, thus fear.

Hence, one must be careful but not be afraid to err
And must not shy away from ventures for that matter
For she is sure to hurt herself by not being able to grow
And could never blame others for her forlorn future

-- Phoenix, AZ; 2/3/2002

Perspectives in Thought Perception

Just as our physical body lives on food stuffs
So does our subtle body live on thought stuffs
And mind and matter build this body together
And are designed to support each other
So, nothing is weird about the thought metabolism

It's universal in this world of law and order
That like natures always bunch together
As oil goes with oil and water with water
But oil and water never mix together
Yet, oils aptly modified, mix with water
Likewise, thoughts materialized become the body
This is how thought metabolism seems to occur

Most focused thoughts are turned into emotion
After passing through allied neural connections
Supporting the making of exact neurotransmitters
As the first vital step past the sense-input
Having distinct vibrations as its own signature
Duly spawned in the Amygdala of the brain
That relays the message to the nearby pituitary
For releasing related hormone into the blood
And carry the same to the far away glands
For making other hormones for further relay
Designed to be recognized by the distant targets
By virtue of the strict receptors the cell-surface hold
To raise the cell-level of some mighty mediators
(Like cyclic AMP, calcium and inositol phosphates)
Or modify certain proteins to alter the gene function
Or do both to bring the cell-events to a just end

By tailoring cellular deeds to fit ones energy-needs
During the process of unbiased-thought perception

Despite so, our ego often grabs an incoming thought
And modify it according to the biases of a man
Prior to its passage along the signaling chain
Showing an emotion other than what it might have been
And it is our habit mind working via the hypothalamus
That in effect dominates the outcome of such reactions

Thus, the pituitary hormones and the neurotransmitters
Along with other hormones and cell-mediators
In conjunction with our habit-ridden ego
Play key roles in our complex mind-body organization
In the chain of events during the processing of information
For the digestion of thoughts into diverse bodily emotions

-- 5/5/03, Phoenix, AZ 85281

Voice of Reason

There is a silent voice in all of us
Known as the voice of reason and compassion
Which upon due consideration
Delegate the power for implementation
Of a given task to an eager person
And this in turn enables the man
To harness enough strength and courage
For the proper task execution, and
The process duly recurs prior to every action

Problems occur when
Emotion supersedes the voice of reason
And turns the mind into confusion
The person then jumps into action
Turning a deaf ear to the voice of reason
And in the aftermath of the episode
A series of disturbing reactions set into motion
And depending on the person's nature
It may appear as, envy, anger, hatred or fear
Or a combination of these reactions

When a person suffers such a reaction
In repeated succession of the same episode
Over and over again
Then the person becomes programmed
In his subconscious mind and starts repeating
The same conduct with least suggestion
Thus, being unable to collect the voice of reason
He turns into a prisoner of own twisted emotion

If any fear factor, for instance, comes into play
Suddenly fear seizes him and be on display
While he suffers helplessly like a child
And lives in frustration in his baffled mind
For days and weeks in agony and pain
That wears him down with time in the end
To a point of ill health and extreme exhaustion

The solution though lays in yoga and meditation
That must be practiced on a regular footing
To cleanse a person's body and the mind
Thus restoring the harmony of mind-body duo
Enabling a man to do what he wants to do
By bringing spontaneity back where it belongs to

-- Phoenix, AZ 85008; 2/2/2002

Work and Worship

Any work performed in a selfless mode
Wins the heart of the friends and foes alike
And opens up the spring of endless bliss
Just rooted in her heart
That surrounds her with an aura of
Fresh morning flowers

Such souls hardly bear any anxiety or fear
As her self remains fixed as one with this universe,
That keeps on feeding love to her innermost heart
Surpassing all forms of human barriers

Her acts of work become her art of worship
The energy of the Universe works at her command
Her ego simply blooms like a lotus in a desert oasis
Inciting everyone from miles around

Her heart's compassion encompasses infinite space
Her intellect shines as the blazing sun
Her true self becomes an end in itself
By quenching the thirst of her ever playful soul
With the never ending music of her own

Written originally in Bengali and subsequently published in my book,
Ek Peyelar Jannya; Academic Press, Calcutta, in 1996, and
translated into English on 4/15/2000; Phoenix, Arizona

OM Poems VI:

On Universal Brotherhood

Celebrate the Divine Spirit
World Youth Day of July 2002

"Tolerance is a matter of religious spirit," says the Pope
This helps to find for some faithful a sense of duty and hope
On this world youth day in our deeply troubled world
When our children are suffering elsewhere
From violence, mistrust, fear and anger
And those who are in the direct line of fire
In holy Jerusalem or Himalayan Kashmir or elsewhere
They forget all feelings of holiness in their terror
While anger and violence quickly take over
As an instinct of survival from looming danger

Such misery is sure to stay with us
As long as we identify with narrow religious sects
Deeming Krishna and Christ as different in heart
And Mohammed or Christ as the only savior;
For such mistaken trusts never stand a deep scrutiny.
Hence, children of this world must read and learn
That deathless Spirit alone is our Soul Divine
Which by nature also Love Divine
And "As many faiths, so many paths"-
Showing due respect to all sacred faiths
As voiced by Sri Ramakrishna and his US emissary Vivekananda:
Two embodiments of olden Vedic wisdom from modern India
And supported by the mystics of all world religions
Upholding the unity of Godhead and universal brotherhood of men
Emphasizing time and time again
Against discrimination among mankind based on cast or creed:
The principle on which the great United States of America was built
By the founding fathers of this great nation with astounding foresight

105

So, religious teachers of the day must teach this truth
That the Omnipresent Spirit alone is the Lord of this universe
And we are the direct progeny of this ONE immortal Soul
Who appears as conditioned souls like us for divine play, and
The great minds of all times in our world
Like Buddha, Christ, Moses and Mohammed
Are the models of what an embodiment of purity could become
So, we must love one another as brothers and sisters
With a spiritual awakening from current slumber
For, it is this sacred celebration of Love that is going to save us:
This ignorant, tense, bewildered humanity from current danger

Happy New Year to All

Hello there! Wherever you are
We wish you all a happy and healthy New Year
Mind you - the children of immortal Soul
Wake up now in your spiritual goal
And live and let live in harmony forever

We all in truth are brothers and sisters:
Offspring of the ONE all-loving ancestor
Whatever you do or where ever you are
We wish you all a very compassionate New Year!

Hey, destroy the tough old habits
Get into Yoga and stay fit
Imbibe all good thoughts and nurture
We wish you all a happy and healthy New Year!

-- January 1, 2004, Phoenix, AZ

Heart-Songs of Mattie Stepanek

Behold the mind-power of this child over own body
This little Mattie Stepanek, a playful prudent soul
An embodiment of pure consciousness even at 12 years old
Fighting a dreadful disease of muscular dystrophy
Yet, so sure of himself as the deathless blissful soul
That he truly lives in divine harmony, free from all worry.

He has the timeliest message for us all
For the ailing mankind of today's edgy world,
That it is a high time to begin a new paradigm
For world-wide peace and mind-body harmony,
Where we must forgo the power of brutal animal force
And embrace love and wisdom to conquer human heart.

Listen to Mattie's Heart-Songs, his beautiful poems
Giving off an aroma of love rich in universal vision,
Echoing from his heart in enchanting words
Like a sweet Vedic hymn, *"Ye children of immortal soul,"*
It rumbles through the veins of love-thirsty humanity
As he invites them to his vision of all-embracing unity

"Just listen to your heart instead of the head," he said
In sharing his vision in Larry King Live in CNN, and
Each of us must be committed to peace, he added
And must want it bad enough to brood over all the time,
Only then will the peace succeed in our heart in the end
Rendering us blissful and blessed in our beloved planet

-- Phoenix, AZ; 9/4/2002

This poem is dedicated to the memory of the child-poet, Mattie Stephanek.. In his short life of 14 years Mattie tirelessly worked towards making this world a better place for all through a series of heart-warming books of poems, called Heart Songs that appropriately hit the recent New York Times best sellers list. He was an undaunted maverick who lived a life of creative joy, ignoring his own terminal illness.

In life you embodied a spirit of love and dignity
In death you have become a spirit of solidarity

Tushar K. Ray
6/26/2004

Seasons Greetings

Riding with our earthen Mother
Going around the sun
I'm back again to the same season
For this holy occasion

I see them all joining the festival
From all around me
The sky, the hills, air and the forests
All are full of glee

The power of our blissful Mother
Is visible all around
In flowers, clouds, sun and bird-songs
Her powerful love is abound

(Hey, brothers and sisters :)
We are here all together
You may believe it or not
Connected by our beloved Mother
All of us have been caught

We all differ in mind-body nature
But as Soul we are the same
We all stem from ONE cosmic Mother
To fulfill Her eternal game

I send you now my greetings of peace
From this part of my world
May you feel the bliss of our Mother
In whatever place you are!

-- Tempe, Arizona October 5, 2003

The Amazing Cosmic Baby

God the absolute is both transcendent and immanent,
Likened to our ego relative to this mind-body outfit
As our transcendent Lord, God is the universal support for all
Creating this universe by His omnipotent energy and will power, and
In His immanent aspect God embodies His creations across the cosmos
Spontaneously evolving in a self-organizing vastly intricate network

Like an innocent baby busy in the spontaneous play of a piano
God is forever playing with this gigantic piano-universe --
Playing with the wills and emotions of His numerous creatures:
Will for fulfilling own desire under the principle of their innate nature
While most are borne by their self-instinct, rest led by their willpower
So as to enjoy a holistic experience in expressing their true feature

In the end, God is the origin of our endless "I- consciousness"
Who has taken both transcendent and immanent roles by divine Will, and
Our will is only a tiny spark of His self-effulgent transcendental willpower
And our body is only a miniature form of His gigantic cosmic body
That holds our own body as a vanishing dot in His vast universal network
Where we are thought to play God's will while attuned to His world music!
By joining our inner rhythm to His amazing world-wide band:
The grand piano of this *Only Cosmic Baby* personifying this vast universe!

-- Tempe, AZ 85281; 10/1/03

The Traveling Monks*

The traveling monks of the 21st Century
Truly happy, truly jolly and freed from most worry
Going places in buses, autos and flying jets
To spread the words of wisdom to curious sentient
And ready to help others in full compassion
They bless all beings along the way

Peace for all is their ultimate goal
Showing us, the confused the path to follow
Which they also trample as living example
So nothing do they say or do are hollow!

Happiness is only a state of the mind, they say
And is an art to grasp the ego-less mind
And to imbibe a thought of happiness for all
Is a sure way to maintain the peace of mind

Selfless love is the only way to peace
Knowing a man's heart is the seat of his Soul
As taught by Krishna, Buddha, and Jesus alike
And live in this modality in words and deeds

-- Phoenix, AZ; 5/27/2002

*Dedicated to All Buddhist and Hindu Monks, and other traveling
Monks of this 21st Century

You Are That

In this vast panoramic universe
The spectacle that we see all around us
Appear so real, but in reality and truth
They are only in part real, hence untruth.

The ultimate reality is our invisible Consciousness
That universal support for all fleeting things
And the true source of all our power and joy within
That can be felt way down in our heart
Past our narrow senses and impure intellect:
She (or He) is our Eternity
Our ageless, sexless and shapeless immortality
Ultimate source of all our knowledge and beauty
That's Her real identity.

She is our Eternal Beloved, and we are
Love Herself encased in this temporal body;
The body made up of energy and information,
Derived from the same material pool
Of infinite creation
Of this universe neighboring us and far beyond

So my friend --
Just let go this idea of material identity
The root cause of all our confused personality
Then what would be left behind is love and beauty
And child-like spontaneity:
A rare mix of absolute wisdom in holistic simplicity
Sustained by the Will of our all-embracing Majesty
Feel that Unity in your heart
Just feel it and become blissfully transfixed
Then you have found your true identity at last
My dear, you are That!

-- Phoenix, AZ; 4/4/01

OM Poems VII:

On Variety Themes

Global Mother Teresa

Oh, mother Teresa--As a missionary you came
To the city of Calcutta as a gift from God
To help the poor and homeless, and
To teach the world by your living example
How to help our own spirit by helping others

In your daily walks of life you saw,
So many hapless and dying people of all ages
That your Mother-Heart could not stand to be aloof
So, you keenly embraced them in your loving bosom.

You saw the plight of the neglected humanity
Of those begging for a little food and attention
Of those who are victims of ill-fates in our society
Getting punished mainly on account of being poor

Being mortally wounded,
By the injustice and aloofness of the society,
You extended your kind hands to the poor and homeless
To provide them the least
They could deserve as the suffering humanity
Like a little food, tiny shelter and a lot of compassion
Thus upholding the cause of the human dignity

You thus light up their mind and soul
And won their heart in return
And saw your beloved Jesus as divine sparks
In the eyes of everyone

This way, Oh Mother,
You demonstrated to the whole world,
That love is the basic means that the world needs
For fixing social injustice and disharmony
At this dawn of a brand-new century

I saw you in the air with your mourning children,
Sleeping like a baby in the mother's arm,
In total communion with your beloved Jesus;
And, in perfect unison with the rest of us

In life, you mostly enlightened
The bosom of Mother-Bengal;
But in death, you have lit up
The bosom of our entire Universe!

This is why we see countless souls
From all the globe over;
The statesmen, the dignitaries and all
From the rich and the poor countries alike
Coming to pay their homage
Bearing faith in your memorable cause

Oh Mother --
I am paying you my passionate homage
From this far-away land
Please accept it and oblige me!

-- Phoenix, Arizona; 9/17/97

Birthday Celebration

Hi there Bengali New Year
Welcome home!
I long for your homecoming
Year after year
On this day in a cyclic manner
And this year
Far away from my birthplace
On this arid land of Saguaro Cactus
In great South Western United States
I welcome you, my dear
Welcome home!

You bring a special joy for me
Each year on this day
When sixty four years ago today
On your long cosmic journey
I joined you as a newborn baby
To be with my beloved mother, and
Then on we are connected to each other
And once each year you greet me
When we celebrate this day
As you bring me fresh spring blossoms
And wish me happy birthday!

-- Phoenix, AZ; 4/14/02

Birthday

Hey, what's so special on this day?
Though I happened to be born
Sixty-five years ago today!

Does it make a cause for celebration?
Am I not born every morning?
Following my restful sleep?
Every night I die of momentary death
Severed from the conscious universe
While dwelling in oblivion!

Why night? Even during the day
I, at times die
In my desires and thoughts
And born again in brand-new hopes and ideas
As I steer across
The countless waves of desires and thoughts
I become the ocean on occasions
Only to be back anew further down

Physical death is equally a passing exit for me
From this ever fleeting body of mine
On to the realm of a new deathless consciousness
To appear again with another nascent body
At separate points along the space-time continuum
For enjoying the beauty of this amazing universe
Anew and afresh
With a brand-new body and senses

So hey, don't just say Happy Birthday today
Wish me happiness every single day!

-- 4/14/2003; Phoenix, AZ 85281

Earth Songs

Does the Sky ever sing the Earth-songs?
Does it store them for future reflection?
Who could tell?
The rainbows keep on singing the Earth-songs
In overflowing love over the multihued horizon
Does the Sky ever keep track of that glory?

Earth-song gushes out on me to please my senses
From all sides, for all times
From cool forest breeze and green meadows
From colorful brooks and mountain shadows
From monsoon rain and the desert winds
They approach me with ever-new tunes
One after another in their usual sequence
Like the waves of an ocean, they resonate my heart
Then dissolve and disappear into the infinite space
Without leaving a clue to its tie with the limitless sky

Does the limitless sky keep track of the limited?
Could anyone fill me on that?
Does fullness ever feel pains for one's emptiness?
Who else could tell but the fullness itself?
May be someday, some one will
By becoming the fullness of sky by himself!

-- Phoenix, AZ 85008; 10/1/2002

Grand Canyon

Come one and come all --
From the comfort of your home
To join this Grand Canyon party
And enjoy this sight of a beautiful night
Of this splendor of darkness
In her grand naive beauty

The echoing wind of this moon-bathed night
Is roaming and roving all around
Tending the heart of the Grand Canyon sight
Where timeless memoirs abound

The bushes and trees over the canyon scene
Are twisting and turning with the wind
As wind keeps on playing this touch and go
By pulling her tricks all around

The pulsating moon over the canyon sky
Is showering her bliss all around
The panorama of stars are playing cool music
In their pompous silent sound

And music of the stones of this mystic canyon
Also joined this symphony tonight
And wind has been lost in her dancing trance
Oh, come on and enjoy this sight!

Oh, come one and come all
From the comfort of your home
To join this festive mood
Tonight is the night of one of a kind
So come on to catch on to this grandeur of sight
Or else, it would be gone for good

-- 6/23/2002; Phoenix, AZ 85008

Kiss

When the river became a dark meadow
And the stars became the lake
And the hooters became the wild terrain
I was waiting for your sake
For you to come in this blissful evening
And be seated by my heart
And to be one with my joyous feeling
Becoming the joy at last
Thus share the bliss from deep within
And arrest the moment in us
Like a mother and baby coming together
Following a time apart
When each in spirit becomes the other
Devoid of commotion what so ever
So let's have such a plunge together
In this ocean of bliss
Like the baby in her mother's bosom
Let our lips be a kiss in unison
By joining the joyous Nature's rhythm
Let's become the bliss!

-- Phoenix, AZ; 2/20/2002

Leela

What really makes you wear this garland
Made of fallen-flowers?
So, you may not have to sever these pure souls
Before their parting hours?

Is that why you linger under the shade
With dancing dews over the lawn
And look up anxious to embrace them
When they would be falling on their own?

The flowers too seem utterly fearless
And eager to fall down free, and
Be in the bosom of their eternal mother
Being free from their motherly tree.

It is only for your deep love, my Beloved,
I am sure in my mind
That the flowers else are so much fearless,
Never bothering to look behind.

Written originally in Bengali on 6/10/1989 (subsequently published in my book, Ek Peyelar Jannya; Academic Press, Calcutta, in 1996), and translated into English in its final form on 4/15/2001; Phoenix, Arizona

Little Garden Flower

Hi there, you make me real happy
As I see your face being light up
Each time you gaze at me by the garden
And offer a note of silent admiration

But I become truly besieged in bliss
When the bees fly straight to me and kiss
Without showing any hesitation
Not even bothering to seek my permission

Hi my friend, you know
I'm much obliged for your taking the time
To be in my presence saying 'hello'
And forever I am thankful to you for saying so

But the bees, as you know
Come to share their fervent love for me
Stealing my heart along the way
Leaving me utterly speechless
Since I don't know what to say
And forever I am thankful to them for doing so

And as for myself being a tiny garden-flower
I am in love with my own tiny universe
Feeling connected to everything here around us
Forever I am grateful and blissful for being so

Written originally in Bengali on 7/29/1988 (subsequently published in my book, Ek Peyelar Jannya; Academic Press, Calcutta, in 1996), and Translated into English in its final form on 1/18/2002; Phoenix, Arizona

New Year 2002

Hi there New Year!
We welcome you as the year 2002!
As we do every year, year after year
Since the reckoning of time
But it seems though you don't care
You come and go at your own pace
With unprecedented grace
And as a silent witness of our Universe
You take truthful notes and gently pass

This rhythm of your eternal dance
Was firmly set at the dawn of creation
That still goes on undaunted
In a cyclic manner in full elegance
And thus in essence
By treading the same path every year
You give the appearance of a new birth
Beginning another fresh year
While you are indeed ageless
And travel at your own rhythmic pace.

For us the mortals
You became the measure of progress
In all aspects of material and spiritual
So that in each year ends
You give us a chance to reexamine
Our past words and deeds
And help us decide any remedial changes
That should be pursued
For personal welfare and collective good

And thus motivate us to be a better being
And make a better world in the end.

With that spirit in mind
Our troubled World eagerly welcomes you
Oh, truly ageless Two Thousand and Two!

-- Phoenix, AZ 85008; 12/24/2001

On My Happy Birthday

Hey, today is my birthday
That's what my mom would say
If she was living on this earth today
"Happy birthday my son!" Because
She gave birth to this body of mine
Sixty-three years ago today!
Perhaps she is wishing my happiness
Right now,
This very moment
From high heavens
Speaking in her soft loving tone
"Happy birthday my son!"

On second thought,
How could I say 'perhaps'?
She must be wishing me that
Since her voice still rings in my ear
And resonates in my vocal chord
Still I can feel her thrill this day
As she did special prayers for me
Year after year for fifty-nine years
Before quitting her mortal body

And last time six years back today
She treated my 57th birthday
With so much love, emotion and care
That even today it is vividly clear
In the deep silence of my heart!
I hear my mom saying
"Happy birthday my son"
Schhh!! Did you hear that?

-- 4/14/2001

Reign of Hope

My Hope came out as an early morning cloud
Hanging over the palm trees around the foothills,
And moist winds roamed like a wandering vagabond
Moving to and fro around the desert valleys
Queen of the valley is she who just came
To quench the April thirst with her eternal game.

At a glance though she appeared just aimless
But not so if seen in kindness
Busy she was nursing the parched young buds
Calming them down with love and kisses

She brought henceforth her music of hope
From sprinkling heavens as the showers
And kindled those hearts with the fires of love
And filled them over in blissful dreams

Desires of the buds to blossom into flowers
Soon began humming in the valley's air, and
The bees were invited to join the celebration,
From distant groves over the naked mountain

That's how our Hope takes care of the valley
In many disguises after the wheel of season
Knowing the needs of all in her desert valley
She pays us visits at the appropriate time.

-- 4/2/2001

The Bird-Symphony

Have you heard
The symphony of the birds
At sundown, dusk and dawn
In a forest lawn?
How do they call your soul
With their heart and soul
From the sacred sanctuary
Of your own?
From the core of their entire being
They incite you to join them
In their joyous singing
Just to see them
Just to feel them
Just to be with them
They would do all the doing
Without any pre-condition
Nothing to bear
Nothing to fear
Only to be with them and share
Their selfless love and care
That's all, nothing more
No demand, no conflict, no sore
Only share their unlimited bliss
And unbounded joy!

-- Phoenix, AZ

The Boy with a Lamp

I saw the little bare-footed boy the other day
In the quietness of a peaceful evening,
Carrying an open lamp on both hands,
And strolling towards me at a soft gentle pace

How could a child have a flaming lamp, I wondered
Being concerned about his safety,
When the child walked up close to me
And held his exquisite eyes on myself

I saw his long silky hair,
Gently brushing his cute little shoulder,
And a serene face, not quite smiling,
But, ready to break out like a desert lightening
In the silence of an early evening storm

"Where did you get this light from?" I asked
He remained quiet for a few long moments
Then blowing the flame out all on a sudden
Asked me in turn with a playful smile,
"Tell me now where the light might have gone?"

Then, after a pause he went on
"I will tell you where I got the light from,
If you would tell me where light is now gone"
With a deep sigh of relief I turned into myself
And sank into the dim twilight for meditation

The Spring

I did hear her silent songs
Behind the fury of our gray winter
Like the comforting note of a loving mother
Hidden under her false anger

Quietly she came on a sudden note
Under the veils of many budding colors
And secretly entered into my own inner heart
Caring less for any formal consent

Out she came of the sleeping seeds
Filling the air with a fragrance indeed
She hugged bare trees as the tender young leaves
And danced over the meadows with dazzling dews

She flung her wings with the flying swans, and
Joined the singing with joyous robins,
And kissing the flowers as cute humming birds,
She formed a symphony all around us

In the midst of all these lovely events
One thought alone became too clear to me
That good old winter has left us alone, and
Playful spring will linger for the time.

-- Phoenix, AZ 85008

Printed in the United Kingdom
by Lightning Source UK Ltd.
127575UK00001B/114/A